Sports Stars

DAN MARINO

Wonder Boy Quarterback

By Bob Rubin

 CHILDRENS PRESS ™

CHICAGO

Cover photograph: Ron Wyatt
Inside photographs courtesy of the following:
Peter Travers, pages 6, 17, and 31
Ira Golden, pages 9, 13, 15, and 25
Vic Milton, page 11
Ray De Aragon, pages 16, 37, and 39
© 1984 Mike Valeri, pages 19, 33, and 41
Bryan Yablonsky, page 21
Michael K. Herbert, page 23
George Gojkovich, pages 27, 29, and 34
Al Kooistra, page 35

Library of Congress Cataloging in Publication Data

Rubin, Bob.
    Dan Marino: wonder boy quarterback

    (Sport stars)
    Summary: A biography of a record-setting quarterback for
the Miami Dolphins, Dan Marino.
    1. Marino, Dan, 1961-   —Juvenile literature.
2. Football players—United States—Biography—Juvenile
literature. 3. National Football League—Juvenile literature.
[1. Marino, Dan, 1961-   . 2. Football players.] I. Title.
GV939.M29R83 1985   796.332'092'4 [B] [92] 85-9724
ISBN 0-516-04347-1
Seventh Printing, 1991
Copyright © 1985 by Regensteiner Publishing Enterprises, Inc.
All rights reserved. Published simultaneously in Canada.
Printed in the United States of America.

    7 8 9 10 R 94 93

Sports Stars

DAN MARINO

Wonder Boy Quarterback

Dan Marino's parents had an idea their son would be an athlete from the time he was just a baby. Everything little Danny saw looked like a ball to him.

"He even called light bulbs balls," says his mother.

Dan's parents were right. He became a star quarterback in high school in Pittsburgh. Then he was an All-American at the University of Pittsburgh. Now he's the best quarterback in the National Football League.

Dan plays for the Miami Dolphins. In 1984, only his second pro season, Dan set many important passing records. He threw for 5,084 yards and 48 touchdowns. No other player had thrown that many yards before. Dan completed 362 passes. Another record. He led the Dolphins to the Super Bowl. They lost to the San Francisco 49ers, 38 to 16.

But it wasn't Dan's fault. The whole Dolphin team played poorly. Dan was only 23 years old. That's very young for a star quarterback in the NFL. Everybody thought he'd get another chance to play in the Super Bowl. Next time, they thought he'd help the Dolphins win.

It usually takes an NFL quarterback many years to learn his position. But Dan learned it right away. That amazed people who know a lot about the game.

Ed Newman plays guard for the Dolphins. He blocks for Dan to give him time to throw his passes. Newman has played for many years and has seen many quarterbacks. He couldn't believe how good Dan became in such a short time.

"I keep saying, 'Pinch me,' but the kid's for real," Newman says.

"Dan Marino's the best quarterback I've ever seen," says Terry Bradshaw. Bradshaw was a star for the Pittsburgh Steelers for many years before he retired. People used to say *he* was the best quarterback they had ever seen.

What makes Dan so good? The most important thing is his strong, accurate arm. When he was a rookie with the Dolphins, he threw a 30-yard touchdown pass against the New York Jets. Dolphin tight end Joe Rose caught the ball in the middle of a group of Jet defenders. Dan's pass had to be perfect. If it hadn't been, it would have been intercepted.

Bob Griese was the best quarterback the Dolphins had before Dan Marino came along in 1983. Marino broke all of Griese's season passing records.

"It's just amazing," Griese says. "Marino went right to the top. How much higher can he go? How much room is there for improvement?"

Bob Griese, Miami's former quarterback, and Dan watch practice.

The ball was thrown like a bullet. Players on both sides marveled.

"I don't think I've ever seen a pass like that," says Dolphin guard Bob Kuechenberg.

Kuechenberg had played for 14 seasons, so he had seen thousands of passes thrown. "One second he's standing back there, and the next second—before you could say, um, Kuechenberg—the ball's in the end zone. It was all of a sudden—like whoosh," Kuechenberg says.

When a quarterback gets rid of the ball in a hurry, they say he has a quick release. It's very important because it makes it hard for tacklers to knock him down before he throws the ball.

Dan gets sacked by Mark Gastineau of the New York Jets.

Dan has a very quick release. It is hard for tacklers to get to him before he throws the ball.

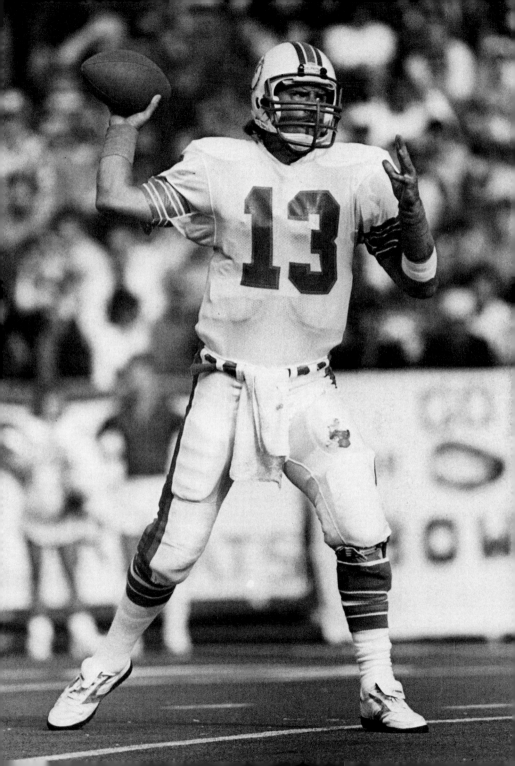

Dan has the quickest release in football. He holds the ball near his ear and flicks his wrist. The ball zips downfield in a perfect spiral.

Dan says his father, Dan Sr., taught him how to do that when he was a boy. Dan's dad worked at night delivering newspapers, so he had time during the day to play with his son.

"I was very lucky to have my dad around all the time," Dan says. "He was my coach."

Father and son played baseball and football. Dan was an excellent baseball player. The Kansas City Royals offered him $30,000 to sign when he graduated from high school. But he liked football better. He also wanted to get a college education.

Dan enjoys playing football.

Dan's dad taught him how to throw a football the right way.

"He taught me to throw without any wasted motion," Dan says. "When you're younger, you don't have the arm strength to throw the right way. But my dad said if I worked on it the right way, I'd be able to throw it a lot better once I got bigger and stronger.

'He made me practice the right way. It was good advice."

Dan started playing quarterback when he was in the fourth grade. He played at St. Regis Elementary School. It was right across the street from his house in Pittsburgh.

Dan loved sports so much he didn't study hard enough. His sixth grade teacher told his parents he would not graduate if he didn't study harder. There was nothing wrong with Dan's brain. It's just that the only thing he was interested in was sports. So he used his brain only for sports.

"Danny could recall everything on a bubble gum card. But he couldn't remember when the Civil War started," his father says.

Dan's father had a talk with him. He told him how important his schoolwork was. Dan listened. He began to study more and his grades improved.

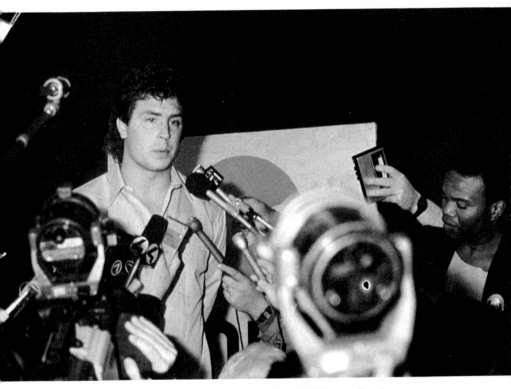

Dan talks to members of the press before the 1985 Super Bowl.

Dan was a happy-go-lucky boy. He enjoyed singing, even though he couldn't carry a tune very well. He watched "Lassie" on television and cried when the collie got in trouble. He brought home a frog and wanted to make a home for it on the back porch.

When Dan was eight, he went fishing with his mother and two younger sisters. He baited his sisters' hooks with worms. Then he told his mother to bait her hook. His mother didn't like touching a live worm, but she did it to make Dan happy. They caught a lot of pan fish.

"Danny was so proud that he taught me to fish," his mother says.

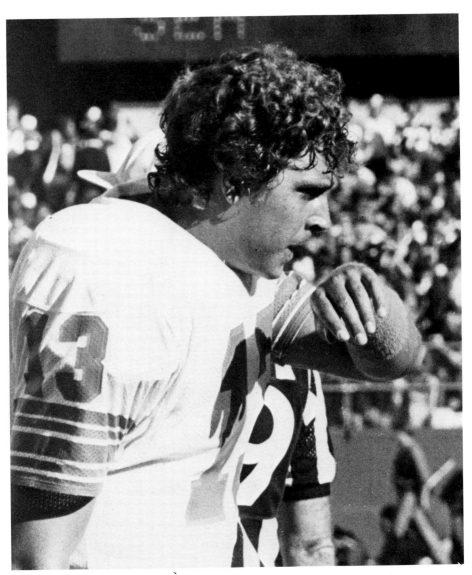

Although Dan is still happy-go-lucky, he is serious about his
job as quarterback.

Dan played quarterback for Central Catholic High School. It was only four blocks from his house. He was so good, colleges from all over the country wanted him to play for them. But he had been born and raised in Pittsburgh. He loved his hometown. So he went to the University of Pittsburgh.

For three years Dan was one of the best college quarterbacks in the country. Pitt won 33 games and lost only three during that time. In his junior year, Dan threw 37 touchdown passes. That was a college record.

But he wasn't as good in his senior year. Neither was the team. Pitt won 9 games, but lost three. Dan's touchdown passes dropped by 20. He had 23 passes intercepted.

Dan talks with University of Pittsburgh teammate Hugh Green. Green played pro ball with the Tampa Bay Buccaneers, then joined Dan's Miami Dolphins. Now they play together again.

But there were reasons for this. Pitt had a new head coach who changed the passing plays. Dan's best receivers had graduated. And Dan was trying too hard. He threw bad passes. He did it because he wanted to score touchdowns and win so badly.

The Pitt fans had cheered him for three years. Suddenly they began to boo him. He didn't like it. It hurt his feelings. But he understood why they were booing.

"I don't think it was a matter of them booing me personally," Dan says. "It was the position I played. At quarterback you get a lot of the credit when things are going well and lot of the blame when they aren't. But football is a team sport. If you lose, it's not all because of one guy.

Dan's feelings were hurt when the Pitt fans booed him.

If you win, it isn't all because of one guy either."

But the problems during his senior year proved to be good luck for Dan. It gave the Miami Dolphins a chance to pick him in the draft.

NFL teams watch college players closely. They want to know who to pick in the draft. Many teams forgot Dan's three great seasons at Pitt. All they remembered was his senior year. So they chose other quarterbacks. They goofed.

Five college quarterbacks were picked before the Dolphins selected Dan. That was great for Dan and the Dolphins. The Dolphins needed a quarterback. That meant Dan would have the chance to play right away. And the Dolphins were a very good team. They had gone to the Super Bowl the year before Dan joined them.

That meant Dan had some very talented teammates.

Dan was very nervous on draft day. He watched television with his family and friends as players were being picked. He wondered when he'd be chosen. He wondered which team would pick him.

"It was one of the toughest days I've ever gone through," Dan says. "You have no idea what's in store for you."

The Dolphins' coach is Don Shula. He is considered one of the greatest coaches in NFL history. He has one of the best records. He studied films of Dan in college and was very impressed.

The Dolphins' coach, Don Shula, and Dan talk about plays.

He was happy to have Dan join the team.

"We had videotapes of all the top quarter-backs and studied their workouts," Shula says. "Every time you looked at Marino setting up and throwing the ball, he was always on target."

Shula made Dan work hard when he reported as a rookie. Dan was glad he did.

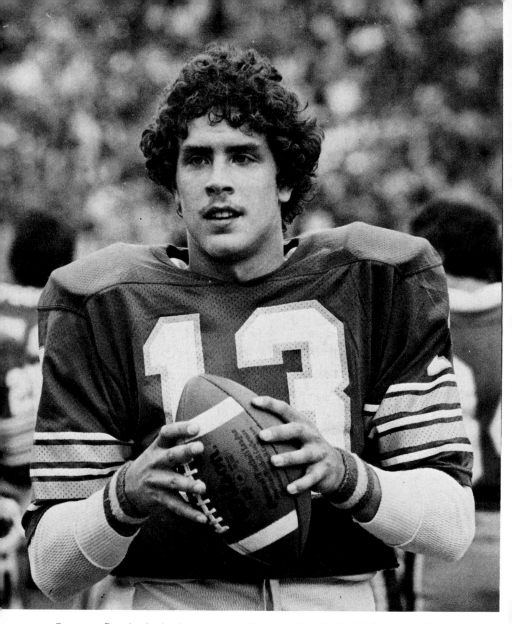

Because Dan had a bad year as a college senior, the Dolphins were able
to pick him in the draft.

"Coach Shula really pushed me in practice," Dan says. "That was good. He made me call my own plays instead of just calling them for me and me just memorizing them. That made me think and study a lot harder."

The studying paid off, Dan threw 20 touchdown passes and had only 6 intercepted. He was named NFL Rookie of the Year. He was the first rookie quarterback ever named a starter in the Pro Bowl game. That's a game played each year after the Super Bowl. It is played between the players voted best in the league by all the other players.

But as good as Dan was in his first season, he was far, far better in his second year. That's when he set all the records.

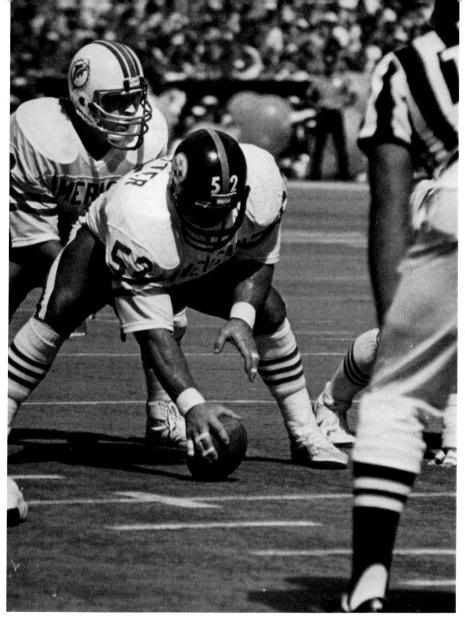

Dan played quarterback in the Pro Bowl Game.

Dan impressed each one of the Dolphins. It wasn't just his playing. It was his friendliness. It was the way he praised his teammates. He wasn't a big shot. He didn't get a swelled head, even after he became a star.

"He's easygoing, the kind of guy you like to sit down and have a beer with and chew the fat," says Dolphin nose tackle Bob Baumhower. "And he hasn't changed from day one. He's a very real person. What you see is what you get. Nothing seems to affect him."

Dan likes children. He arranged to have free shoes given to children whose fathers were out of work in Pittsburgh. He arranged to have free T-shirts given to needy children in Pittsburgh

Nat Moore (39) and Bud Brown (43) talk to Dan on the sidelines.

and Miami. He works with retarded children in the Special Olympics. He also was national chairman of a fun run to benefit people with muscular dystrophy. That's a disease that cripples youngsters and adults alike.

So Dan is a fine person as well as a great quarterback. What players and fans all want to know is what other records he will break before he's finished playing football. One player says there should be two record books. One would be for Dan, and one for the rest of the league.

Dan doesn't think about setting records. He's more interested in helping his team win.

"All I want to do is work as hard as I possibly can," he says. "That way, when I'm finished playing, I'll know I was as good as I possibly could have been."

In 1986, Dan continued to set records. Now there was no question. He is one of the greatest

Dan is a fine person as well as a great quarterback.

quarterbacks ever to play football. He won All-NFL honors, was the NFL Players Association Alumni player of the year, and the Seagram's player of the year. Everyone voted him on their All-NFL team.

In 1986 Dan finally attempted more than 1,500 passes. That meant he could be rated on the all-time rating list. Guess where he was rated? That's right, he was No. 1!

Dan had three 400-yard passing days in 1986. He set an NFL record with seven 400-yard passing days. He was the only quarterback to throw a touchdown in every game in 1986.

But Dan had another fine thing happen to him in 1986. That was the birth of his first son, Daniel Charles Marino. Dan and his wife, Claire, are very happy.

In 1987 Dan is called the second-best quarterback in the American Conference. In 1989 he was rated leading lifetime passer. And in 1991 Dan again was a National Football League leader with an overall rating of 82.6, with 531 attempts, 306 completes, and 21 touchdown passes.

In his tenth season, in 1992, Dan was credited with making 129 consecutive starts, more than any quarterback since the 1970 merger of the NFL and AFL—even starting a number of times with injuries through this streak.

In the 1992-1993 season Dan's record of touch-down passes assisted the Dolphins in reaching the championship AFC divisional playoffs, although they lost the last game to the Buffalo Bills. Dan was once again a National Football League statistical leader with an overall rating of 85.1, making 554 attempts, 330 completes, and 24 touchdown passes.

Dan has worked very hard. He is the very best.

CHRONOLOGY

1961 —Dan Marino is born on September 15 in Pittsburgh.

1970 —Dan starts to play quarterback at St. Regis Elementary School.

1977-78—Dan throws for 2,800 yards in two years at Central Catholic High School. He is an all-city pick.

1979 —Dan rejects a $30,000 offer from the Kansas City Royals to play baseball. He enrolls at the University of Pittsburgh.

1979-82—Dan completes an All-American four-year career at Pitt. He completes 693 passes in 1,204 attempts for 8,597 yards and 79 touchdowns.

1983 —Dan is drafted by the Miami Dolphins on April 26. He is the sixth quarterback selected, and the 27th player overall.

—Dan starts his first NFL game on October 9. He throws for 322 yards and three touchdowns in a loss to the Buffalo Bills.

—In December, Dan is voted the first starting rookie quarterback in the 1984 Pro Bowl.

1984 —In January, Dan is named NFL Offensive Rookie of the Year.

—Dan breaks the Dolphin single-game passing yardage record with 429 on September 30. It happens in a victory over the St. Louis Cardinals.

—Dan breaks the league record of 36 touchdown passes in one season. He throws four for a total of 40 in a loss to the Los Angeles Raiders on December 2.

—Dan breaks the league record for season passing yardage (4,802). He throws for 340 yards in a season-closing victory over the Dallas Cowboys on December 17. It gives him a total of 5,084.

—Dan is named the Most Valuable Player in the NFL just after the season ends.

1985 —In January, Dan leads the Dolphins to the Super Bowl.

1985-86—Dan passes for 4,137 yards, the fourth-best quarterback in the American Conference.

1987   —Dan passes for 3,245 yards completing 263 of 444 attempts and 26 touchdowns, the second-best quarterback in the American Conference.

1988-89—Dan is rated the leading lifetime passer with a rating of 94.1 points and wins the PRO-AM title with a best ball total of 255.

1989-90—Dan is the National Football League's 1989 statistical leader with an overall rating of 76.9 points; he completes 308 of his 550 attempts, gains 3,997 yards and makes 24 touchdown passes.

1990-91—Dan is a National Football League statistical leader for the American Conference with an overall rating of 82.6, with 531 attempts, 306 completes, and 21 touchdown passes.

1992   —In his tenth season, Dan is credited with making 129 consecutive starts, more than any quarterback since the 1970 merger of the NFL and AFL.

1992-93—Dan's record of touchdown passes assists the Dolphins in reaching the championship AFC divisional playoffs, although they lose the last game to the Buffalo Bills. Dan is once again a National Football League statistical leader with an overall rating of 85.1, making 554 attempts, 330 completes and 24 touchdown passes.

ABOUT THE AUTHOR

Bob Rubin has worked for the *Miami Herald* for 8 years. He has covered many sports and major events, including the Super Bowl, the World Series, and the Professional Basketball Championships. He has watched Dan Marino play every game for the Dolphins.

He has written 13 books on sports. They include biographies of Pete Rose, Lou Gehrig, and Ty Cobb, and histories of the Green Bay Packers and Minnesota Vikings. He has a column each month in *Inside Sports*. He also has written numerous magazine articles about different athletes. A column he wrote for the *Miami Herald* was judged best in the nation in 1981 by a panel of sports editors.

Mr. Rubin is married and has two daughters. His hobbies are reading, listening to music, and swimming.